# The ESL Teacher's Guide to South Korea

## KATRINA BAUMANN

# DEDICATION

For everyone who has an adventurous spirit and the courage to follow their dreams overseas

# TABLE OF CONTENTS

# ACKNOWLEDGMENTS

First and foremost, I'd like to thank my family for always being so supportive of all my endeavors and adventures. I couldn't have done it without you. Special thanks to Brant for encouraging me to write and pursue the things I am passionate about. Thank you Ian for reading and editing this guide and providing thoughtful and constructive criticism. A very special thanks to all of the people I met and befriended while living in Korea - I will never forget the incredible experience we all shared together in that strange little piece of land in Northeast Asia. I'd like to thank 임상미 for everything you taught me while we worked together, and all the students who touched my heart and changed my life forever.

# TOP 10 REASONS TO TEACH IN KOREA

1. Moving to Korea is a real adventure. You don't often get a chance in life to move abroad and live amongst a foreign culture - and get paid to do so. The food is really good and almost everything is extremely cheap, so you can live it up for next to nothing. It's a really cool feeling when you finally realize you don't feel like a tourist anymore.

2. Jobs in Korea pay pretty well and it's a great opportunity to pay off student loans and/or credit card debt. If you are smart with your money, you can easily save at least a thousand dollars a month, which you can apply towards bills back home. I know of quite a few people who have paid off all their student loans after a year or two in Korea. I was able to pay off my $6,000 of credit card debt in less than six months!

3. If you're hoping to make a career out of ESL, Korea is the perfect place to start. You don't need any experience for a lot of the jobs that you'll find and in a couple years you can apply for university positions which pay well and offer several months of vacation. If you don't want to stay in Korea forever, having a few years of teaching experience can open a lot of doors to higher paying positions in the Middle East and beyond.

4. Almost every teaching job in Korea offers great perks like free roundtrip airfare and a free apartment. Once you're in Korea, you won't have to worry about finding an apartment and dealing with a lease - it's all done for you before you ever set foot in the country.

5.  Teaching in Korea will help your resume stand out. It might not add value, per se, but in my experience it has definitely been noticed. Each time I've had an interview since leaving Korea it's the first thing that comes up. Everyone wants to know what it was like, or they know someone who has also taught in Asia. In today's global economy, you need something on your resume to help you stand out from the crowd.

6.  If your goal is to travel, working in Korea can help you cross a bunch of things off your bucket list. There are dozens of countries located within an eight hour flight from Korea, so use your vacation time to soak up the sun in Thailand or the Philippines, see the ancient temples of Angkor Wat, hike the Great Wall of China, or discover the jungles of Borneo.

7.  Korea is a very safe country to live in. While crime does occur, it is definitely less common than the crime rates in a lot of large Western cities. I could count on one hand the number of people I knew who taught in Korea who were victims of any kind of crime, let alone violent crime. I never once felt unsafe living in Korea.

8.  Korea is never boring! There is always something going on, and even everyday life in your neighborhood will be entertaining. So many bizarre things happen on a regular basis in Korea. I lived across the street from a karaoke bar, a barbeque restaurant and a pool hall and sometimes I would just stand in my window and watch the drunk salarymen stumble out and try to make their way back home. I also enjoyed taking long walks through my part of town and just people watching. If you make an effort to leave your apartment, you will rarely be bored.

9. Being on your own in a foreign country for even just a year will teach you more about yourself than a decade at home. I went to Korea so I could see the world and save money, but in hindsight that was the least valuable part about my time in the country. I had to take care of myself over there. I had to adapt to a culture that was very different, I had to figure out how to get around the country, how to buy things from stores and restaurants, and how to feel comfortable in my own skin. You spend a lot of time alone, and you get to know yourself in a way that's hard to put into words. By the time you leave, you will feel like you can handle anything life throws at you.

10. Teaching in Korea is an experience you will never forget.

.

# AUTHOR'S NOTE REGARDING MONEY

Throughout this book I often refer to prices in Korean Won. All prices are compared to US Dollars. A lot of recruitment websites say ₩1,000 = $1.00 US but that is not the case and has not been in many years. The exchange rate is always changing, but it's been consistently around ₩1,100 to the dollar. Therefore, if I say something is ₩400,000 you should convert it assuming the won is at 1,100. So ₩400,000 = $355.76.

For up to date conversion rates, check out www.xe.com

# FORWARD

When I graduated from college in 2008, I applied to teach English in South Korea. I had a friend who was teaching in Korea - don't we all know someone doing that these days? - and it seemed like a lot of fun and a great adventure before settling down and starting life in the "real world". I was accepted by the English Program in Korea (EPIK) to teach English in a public elementary school. I was elated and enthusiastic and, most of all, completely terrified! How would I get by in Korea? Their street signs were all just funny characters and their language completely incomprehensible. What kinds of things would I need to know to survive?

I spent hours each day scouring the internet, looking for answers. There are some great resources out there that can answer a lot of your questions, I'll admit that. But there was no book available on the topic. I wanted something that would address all of my questions and give me advice on things I didn't even know I would have to think about. I went over to Korea in August 2009, wishing such a book existed.

Fast forward to 2013; I was doing research on Korea for a novel I was planning to write. While reading about some of the places I was researching, the thought came to me: I wonder if anyone has written a book about what to expect as an ESL teacher in Korea yet? Surely someone has. So I did a search and was surprised to find that there still wasn't much out there. I did find one book on this topic, but it was written in 2001. One thing you will find out once you get to Korea is that a lot will change really fast. One of Korea's slogans was *Dynamic Korea*, and it was completely apt. In just two months, a whole neighborhood had been erected near my apartment where a rice paddy had once been. Not to mention the fact that the ESL industry has exploded in recent years. More foreigners mean more changes, more western foods, restaurants, clothing stores, and activities. A book from 2001 is practically ancient Korean history.

Before we begin, I want to confess something which may sound weird coming from the author of a guide to thriving in Korea - I didn't enjoy living in Korea as much as I should have. At the time, Korea was just the means to an end. I wanted to travel and the money I was earning in Korea helped me do that. I spent so much time looking forward that I didn't stop to enjoy the life I had made in Korea. Every day that passed was a day closer to exiting the country for good. Time for weekend adventures with friends was quickly coming to an end. It wasn't until the spring when I finally realized this. For most of you, your time in Korea is finite. You'll stay one, maybe two, years. Only a few of you will stay long-term, and it's probably because you married a Korean. Once I realized this, my outlook changed and I really began to take advantage of the wild, wacky, strange, beautiful and fun things that make up everyday life in the Land of the Morning Calm. There's not a day that goes by that I don't think about my time in Korea and if I was given the chance to teach ESL abroad again, I would take it in a heartbeat.

So, dear readers, I am writing this for you. I want you to start out on the right foot. I want you to know what you're getting yourself into, and all the potential fun you can have. I want you to be able to go into a restaurant with a Korean menu and be able to start eating and drinking like a pro. I want you to take every advantage you can when you start your new life in Korea. I also want you to be prepared for some of the not-so nice aspects of life in Korea. There are times when you'll get sick or you'll get homesick or lonely. It would be a disservice for me to write a book just about the good parts of life in Korea and then you would get there and be disappointed in your experience. That would be a real shame.

For most of you, the decision to go to Korea is super exciting and really, really nerve wracking. You know it's going to be an adventure, but you also know you're about to jump head first into a country that is so 180 from the place you're from you might as well be going to Mars. My hope is that this guide will answer some of your most pressing concerns.

# 1 - BEFORE YOU GO

*I was such a ball of nerves before I left for Korea. I spent hours reading online about all of the things that could go wrong. I overanalyzed everything. In the end, I brought over two fifty pound suitcases with me, along with a carry-on duffel bag. And that was just my summer clothing. My parents shipped my winter clothes to me once it started getting cold. Trust me on this: you do not need to bring this much stuff. Much of what I brought I ended up not using at all and then I had to pay to ship it back home before I left. So don't make the same mistakes I made when packing your bags for your stint in Korea:*

- If these names don't sound familiar to you yet, they will after you get to Korea- Home Plus, E-mart, Lotte Mart. Think of them as Korea's answer to Target or Wal-Mart superstores. You will find almost everything you could possibly need for groceries and home décor-and they're open 24 hours.

- Don't waste your time and luggage weight allowance on bringing lots of shoes with you. A lot of schools and even restaurants don't want you to wear shoes indoors (it's an Asian thing-you'll figure this out quickly). Even if they don't make you wear slippers to class, they probably won't care what your shoes look like. To be on the safe side, you could bring one or two pairs of dress shoes just in case you need to meet your students' parents or get invited to some sort of fancy party.

I brought about fifteen pairs of shoes, including four or five pairs of high heels. I think I wore four of the shoes I brought: flip flops, running shoes, furry boots, and a pair of dressier flat sandals. I thought I would need high heels for going out, but that is simply not the case. Most popular foreign hangouts are more like a bar on a college campus instead of a dress-to-impress club. The floors will be sticky and wet and someone will probably spill beer on you at some point.

- My mom bought me a ten pack of toothbrushes to take with me. But I was going to Korea, not a tribe deep in the Amazon. Koreans brush their teeth and use toothpaste! All the time! My Korean co-teachers even had toothbrushes in their desks at work. You may want to bring some toothpaste with you if you require a special kind, like for sensitive teeth, but toothpaste is readily available in all stores. You can even find Western brands at the bigger chain grocery stores and Costco.

- There is a lot of debate on ESL message boards about whether you should bring bed sheets with you. True, it can be hard to find fitted sheets, but it's not impossible anymore. However, unless you know how big your bed will be before you go, you may want to hold off on buying that 1,000 thread count queen size bedding set. I spent my time in Korea in a twin size bed with Mickey and Minnie on the headboard. You could always get your family to ship your sheets after you arrive.

- Ladies, you may want to bring some shaving cream with you. Korean women are partial to hair removal creams over shaving, so it can be extremely difficult to find shaving cream that isn't made for men.

- There is also some debate on whether or not you should bring sunscreen. I say bring some. In my experience, most of the sunscreens have skin bleach in them. I have heard of people finding sunscreen that is normal, but they said it wasn't very waterproof and they ended up getting burned after swimming.

- Girls, bring tampons. They can be hard to find and expensive. Also, if your bra size is bigger than a B, you'll probably want to bring some extra bras with you. Korean bras are small. I was never able to find one in my size.

- If you're really tall, or overweight, you will probably have a lot of problems finding clothing that fits. Koreans, as a whole, are small people. I was a good 1-2 heads taller than most of the Korean women I knew and I could never find shirts that were long enough to cover my stomach, or pants that were long enough to cover my legs. One time, early on, I wanted to try on a dress. The girl at the shop literally laughed at me and took the dress out of my hand and wouldn't let me try it on.

- Bring a towel or two for your bathroom. Korean towels are really small (think the size of your t-shirt) and feel rough on your skin.

- Don't bring things like plug-in alarm clocks and hair dryers. You can find them in all the big stores. Plus, your hair dryer won't work properly, even if using a converter.

- Speaking of converters, you'd be wise to bring a couple with you. While you can find them in the big stores, you might not be able to go shopping for the first few days and you'll definitely want to be able to plug in your laptop at home or wherever you are staying during orientation.

- Bring money with you, preferably around $1,000 if you can swing it. You may not get your first paycheck for a month and credit cards aren't always accepted. It's better to bring too much money than too little. You don't want to spend your first month living off of ramen noodles and tap water, do you?

- While you're at it, you might want to bring a pillow. Korean pillows are really uncomfortable!

- If you really don't want to pack a lot, and you're not sure you want to try to navigate the Korean shops to furnish your place when you first arrive, check into TheArrivalStore.com. You can get packages with all of the essentials delivered to you when you arrive. The prices are a bit high, but if convenience is your thing, you should definitely look into them.

- Bring electronics like your laptop or iPod. Before I went, I was under the impression that electronics would probably be super cheap as Korea produces a lot of electronics and they are so close to Japan, which also makes a lot of electronics. I couldn't have been more mistaken. Electronics cost significantly more than you would probably pay at home.

# 2 - GETTING THERE

*So you've decided to come to Korea. You chose your city, you have your visa, you have your contract with your school, and you have all your earthly possessions with you. You check your bags and get on the plane for the twelve-plus hours flight. You arrive at Incheon International Airport and you walk off the plane. Now what?*

- Going through customs in Incheon is easy. The customs agents all seem to speak English and they'll just check to make sure you have your visa in your passport, and then they'll wave you through.

- Make sure you change your money! You can change your money at home, although not all banks and airports will carry Korean won. The airport you are flying from direct to Incheon should have what you need since they service the country. Your other option is to change your money in Korea since they will obviously have their own currency. However, you may want to change your money before you get to Korea just in case your flight gets in late or the airport is really busy and you need to meet up with someone. If you haven't changed money before, don't worry, it's very simple. Just give them the amount of your currency that you would like converted, and they'll give you won in exchange. They may need to see your passport first, so have that handy before you get up to the window.

- You should be met at the airport by someone. If you're working in a hagwon (private school), the school director will meet you at the airport. If you're working in the public school program, EPIK, there will be program coordinators waiting at the airport. Check in with them and then they'll direct you to the appropriate bus, which will take you to wherever your orientation will be held.

- If you're in a private school, you'll be taken to your apartment the first day. If you're with the public school program, you'll be taken to whatever city is holding that season's orientation (ours was in Jeonju, a couple hours away from Seoul). Everyone will have to have a health check the first week they are there. Private schools will have you to the local hospital to get your health check. EPIK brings the health check to you and everyone in the program comes at different times during the day. They'll be checking the basics like height, weight, hearing and eyesight. They'll also draw blood to test for HIV, tuberculosis, and illegal drugs. If you take medication, make sure it won't show up as a false positive! If you test positive for drugs or HIV or tuberculosis you will be deported. If you have a medical check at home, that's fine, but they'll make you do another one in country, no matter what. You'll be expected to cover the cost of the medical check (mine was around $70) and it will either be deducted from your first check or you will have to pay for it out of pocket. Make sure you have enough money to cover it!

**Words to Know About Your Neighborhood**

Province: Do
Counties: Gun
Districts: Gu
Cities: Si
Neighborhoods: Dong
City Blocks: Beonji
Building Number: Ho

# 3 – SETTLING IN

*When you first arrive to your new home in Korea, it will be a pretty overwhelming experience. Not only are you alone in a foreign country where you (probably) can't read the street signs or communicate, but you also have to learn your way around your neighborhood and figure out how to get around town. But with a little planning, you can ease into your new Korean life a little bit faster.*

- Before you do anything else, have your co-teacher or director (we'll call them your Handler from now on) write down your address in Korean. Make copies of your address just in case you lose the original. I cannot stress this enough. In the early months, sometimes showing the cab driver my address in Korean was the only reason I was able to get back home. Even if you know the name of the area in which you live, Korean taxi drivers may not be able to understand what you're saying. If you can hand them your address it will make your rides home much easier!

- Ask your handler to show you how to get to the closest supermarket (Home Plus, E-mart or Lotte Mart). Even if you have a convenience store or small local grocery store nearby, find out how to get to one of these larger stores. You will be frequenting these stores a lot, especially if you are the first person to live in your apartment and you have to buy almost everything to make the place livable.

- Get a Costco membership. Costco has popped up in most major cities now and the membership is good at any store. You'll be able to find so many Western items at Costco that you won't find anywhere else in Korea from Jelly Belly to Tampax to Dr. Pepper. More on Costco later...

- You would be wise to print out maps of your city. An even better idea is to print out maps of the subway lines and/or the bus routes. Until you get the hang of it, public transportation can be a daunting experience! Also find out when the last bus/subway departs from where you're at. If you live far from where you're hanging out, you could be in for an expensive cab ride.

- If you're tight on won but need to furnish your apartment with the basics, check out a store called Daiso 다이소, Korea's ₩1,000 store. Daiso is a Japanese chain dollar store that has over 800 locations all around Korea, including subway stations. You will be amazed at the variety of things you can find at Daiso, as well as the price. I don't care who you are, getting a set of plates and cups for less than $10 is a pretty big deal! But Daiso is not just limited to kitchen and bath accessories; you can get everything from stationary to pet supplies, all for a low, low price.

- Invest in a water filtration pitcher or stock up on bottled water. Korean tap water is terrible and there's a lot of debate on whether it's actually safe to drink long-term. I drank it for about a month before I started hearing that it might not be so good for you. I never got sick from it, but it did taste bad! Don't fear though-bottled water is really cheap. My favorite kind was DMZ water.

# 4 – LEARNING THE KOREAN ALPHABET

*Learning to read the Korean alphabet, called Hangul* 한글, *may sound intimidating at first but it's really quite easy. Unlike Chinese, which has thousands of symbols involved in their writing, the Korean alphabet has only 24 letters. You may not be able to understand what you are reading, but the ability to read a sign or a menu will make your life a lot easier! Carry this page with you when you're out and try to practice reading when you're on public transportation or waiting in lines. You'll find it will only take a few hours before you start to really comprehend what you are looking at!*

*Chart on the following page.*

## The Korean Alphabet

| | | | | | | | |
|---|---|---|---|---|---|---|---|
| ㄱ *G or K* | ㄴ N | ㄷ D or T | ㄹ L or R | ㅁ M | ㅂ B or P | ㅅ S | ㅇ Ng or silent |
| ㅈ J | ㅊ Ch | ㅋ K | ㅌ T | ㅍ P | ㅎ H | ㄲ Kk | ㄸ Tt |
| ㅃ Pp | ㅆ Ss | ㅉ Jj | ㅏ A | ㅑ Ya | ㅓ eo | ㅕ Yeo | ㅗ O |
| ㅛ Yo | ㅜ U | ㅠ Yu | ㅡ eu | ㅣ I | ㅐ ae | ㅒ Yae | ㅔ e |
| ㅖ ye | ㅘ Wa | ㅙ Wae | ㅚ oe | ㅝ Wo | ㅞ We | ㅟ Wi | ㅢ ui |

## Words to Know About Food

*Before you can tackle eating out, you first need to know a few key vocabulary words so you can understand what you're eating.*

**Bap** – Rice
**Galbi** – Marinated beef or pork short ribs
**Gogi** – Meat
**Jjigae** - Stew
**Kim** – Seaweed
**Kimchi** – Spicy fermented cabbage served with every meal
**Maeun (*may-oon*) or Jjalishan** – Spicy
**Mul (*pronounced like mool)* –** Water
**Ppang** – Bread
**Samgyeopsal** – Literally means three layered meat, popular pork dish at Korean BBQ joints
**Sengseon** – Fish
**Tang** – Soup

# 5 – MASTERING THE 'ORANGE RESTAURANT' MENU

*Ah, the ubiquitous orange restaurants. Every neighborhood has at least one. They're very easy to spot as they're orange and usually have some sort of cartoon characters on the front of the store. They'll also have 김밥 (kimbap) somewhere in the name. The orange restaurants are fast food Korean style and you'll be hard pressed to find anything that costs more than ₩5,000. Here's the catch though- it's all in Korean. Unlike other Korean restaurants which are more formal and focus on one type of food, the orange restaurants have a little bit of everything. When I first got to Korea, I was really craving some bibimbap (a delicious rice dish, which you will learn more about shortly). The only problem was, I didn't know where to find it. At the time, I couldn't read any Korean and I had no idea which restaurants had it and which didn't. A few weeks later, I mentioned to my co-teacher that I really wanted bibimbap but couldn't find any. She looked at me like I was crazy and said I could get it right across the street at the orange restaurant. That evening, I mustered up the courage to enter the shop and I ordered my first thing off the menu. It was delicious and only cost ₩4,000! Once I learned how to read Korean and learned what the different foods were called, I ate there almost every night.*

*There are so, so many items on the menu at these restaurants and some offer more variety than others so it's difficult to give you the full menu rundown, but I'll help you with the basics.*

| Hangul | Romanized | Description |
|---|---|---|
| 김밥 | *Kimbap* | Rice wrapped with seaweed (like sushi). Many varieties available including cheese, tuna, beef and vegetable |
| 불고기 덮밥 | *Bulgogi* | Delicious meat marinated in soy sauce, garlic, sugar and sesame oil. Served with rice (my personal favorite orange restaurant dish) |
| 치킨 까스 | *Chickenkass* | Fried chicken cutlet (yes, chicken is pronounced the same in English & Korean) |
| 비빔밥 | *Bibimbap* | White rice mixed with assorted vegetables, spicy Korean pepper paste and often with meat and an egg on top. So good! |
| 돈까스 | *Dongkass* | Fried port cutlet |
| 탕수육 | *Tang Su Yuk* | Korean style sweet and sour pork |
| 김치찌개 | *Kimchi Jjigae* | Spicy kimchi stew |
| 갈비탕 | *Galbi Tang* | Spicy beef soup |
| 신 라면 | *Shin Ramyeon* | Ramen |
| 찐만두 | *Jjin Mandu* | Steamed dumplings |
| 군만두 | *Gun Mandu* | Fried dumplings |
| 우동 | *Udong* | Japanese udon soup |

# 6 - DRINKING

*Drinking in Korea is practically a national pastime. You cannot walk a block without passing a bar of some sort, and the only restaurants I can think of that don't serve alcohol are the aforementioned 'orange restaurants' and fast food places. In Korea it is literally cheaper to buy a bottle of soju at a convenience store than it is to buy a bottle of soda. If you struggle with alcohol I strongly urge you to reconsider going to Korea. The drinking culture permeates every facet of Korean life. This is bad for recovering alcoholics, but great for anyone who likes to go out on a Saturday night (or any other night during the week). Welcome to the world of Korean alcohol:*

- **Soju ( 소주 ):** Think of Soju as Korean vodka. It's clear, it's potent and it's dirt cheap and sold anywhere and everywhere. You can get a bottle of soju from any convenience store for less than $2. You can shoot it or mix it. If you're in a pinch, try mixing it with Chilsung Cider (**칠성사이다**), which tastes like a mixture of ginger ale and lemon lime soda. You can also find flavored soju at bars. Try the kiwi soju - it's delicious. Korean bars aren't really strict and I've found that you can BYO soju to add some kick to your flavored mix.

- **Beer ( 맥주 maegju ):** There's not a lot of explaining to do here. The main brands are Cass and Hite. Like soju, you can get beer cheaply almost anywhere you go. However, if you have the choice between a cheap Korean beer and a more expensive import, you may want to splurge a bit. Korean beer doesn't have a good reputation for great taste. Just sayin'…

- **Makgeolli ( 막걸리 ):** My absolute favorite alcoholic beverage in Korea! Makgeolli (you will see it spelled makkoli a lot online) is a milky rice wine that has a bit of a yeasty aftertaste, sort of like beer but much more delicious, in my opinion. You can get plastic bottles of makgeolli at convenience and grocery stores, but the best is to be found at makgeolli bars. It will be served either in a bowl with a ladle or in a gold kettle. It is best paired with pancakes called pajeon 파전, which are made with eggs, flour, green onions and other toppings, if you so desire. It is the most delicious combination of food and drink. HOWEVER…please heed my advice and do not keep drinking it just because it tastes so good. It's pretty strong stuff and you'll more than likely get a good buzz going after a cup or two. One time, my friend and I went out on a Friday night for a kettle at our local bar. Between the two of us, we usually consumed one kettle and we'd be sufficiently drunk. We were finishing up our drinks when a group of older Korean men next to us began talking to us. They didn't speak much English, but appreciated us talking to them anyway. To show their appreciation, they ordered us another kettle and pajeon. We really didn't need another kettle, but we drank it anyway because we didn't want to be rude. BIG mistake on my part. I could barely walk home from the bar and when I did get there, I was sick all night long. I couldn't eat for three days afterward. I threw up so much I got a sinus infection and woke up the next morning with my eyes full of green gunk. It was not a nice feeling. So don't make the same mistake I did. Drink makgeolli responsibly!

# 7 – MAKING FRIENDS

*One of the hardest parts about going to Korea is that you have to leave your friends and family behind, and nobody likes being alone. I was lucky enough to have gone over with a friend, so at least I had someone in the early days before I started meeting other people. Korea can be a really lonely place if you don't have a social life. But fortunately for you, there are thousands of other people who are in the exact same situation. You just need to know how to find them.*

- Make friends at your school or at orientation. This is a no-brainer. When I went over for EPIK orientation, there were hundreds of us English teachers attending at the same time. Everyone is excited and eager to meet people and make friends. If you're not going into the public school system, you'll more than likely be working with several other foreign teachers at your academy. Have them show you the ropes and get together for dinner or a night out on the town, which leads into point number two…

- You will probably meet a lot of friends through your friends and/or co-workers. Never underestimate how important networking is in Korea. You're all in the same boat: away from home, alone, trying to make friends. For the most part, people are really friendly and eager to set up future activities with you.

- The Internet is a great way to meet like-minded individuals. There are tons of Facebook and Meetup.com groups you can join for all different interests. Like rock climbing? There's a group for that (Sanirang dot net). Like to write? There's a group for that. Like to go out at night and try new places? There's a group for that.

- I met some really great people volunteering to do dog walks at the animal shelter in Daegu. Not only was I meeting new people, but I felt good about helping out at the shelter. In the end, I even ended up adopting one of the dogs I walked! I knew a lot of people who also volunteered at the local orphanage on Sunday afternoons.

- If you're looking to make friends and learn some Korean, take some language classes. Everyone in Korean class will be foreign teachers, so again, you'll all be happy to meet new people to hang out with. A lot of people would go out together for dinner or drinks after class ended.

# 8 - DATING

*There really isn't that much to say about the topic of dating in Korea. You'll meet people the same way you'll meet friends in Korea: work, bars, through friends, joining clubs and groups. There are a few points I'd like to touch on regarding dating, though:*

- Don't go into your life in Korea expecting to find your soul mate. Sure, it *can* happen, but most likely it won't. I'll admit, part of me was very hopeful that I would meet someone special in Korea. What a great story to tell the kids about how mom and dad met, right? But in reality, most people aren't looking for anything serious. The vast majority of teachers are in their twenties and looking to have some fun for a year or two before going home. Casual hookups are extremely common. ESL teachers come from many different backgrounds and countries, and getting too emotionally involved would just be too complicated in the long run. What happens if you do meet someone but you're from different countries? What if you meet someone who is planning to stay for another year but you want to go home after one?

- If you meet someone who's planning to stay another year but you aren't, life becomes extremely complicated. Trust me, I know from experience. I started a romance shortly before I left

Korea, but he was still staying another year so he could pay off some more of his student loans and finish his master's degree. I left and he stayed. We Skype chatted almost every day, which was difficult as there was a major time difference and someone would always have to wake up early and the other would stay up late so we could talk. In the end, it didn't work out. It's hard to carry on a long distance relationship when you aren't even on the same continent. It's certainly not impossible for a relationship to withstand the time apart, but it does make things much harder.

- If you meet a nice Korean guy or girl, be prepared to be flexible. I know many people who dated/are currently dating Koreans and they're very happy. However, our cultures are very different and there's a lot of learning involved. Korean families are very tight knit for the most part and it's common to feel like an outsider as the only non-Korean in the family. However, once you gain their trust and are around long enough, the family will treat you as one of their own and will protect and care for you at all costs. It is important to remember, though, if you do end up marrying a Korean one of you is going to have to live away from your family, friends, and culture. It's a lot more give and take than a relationship in your home country.

# 9 – FUN, KOREAN STYLE

*So you really like going out at night with your friends, but you're a little over the bar scene, or maybe you just want some variety. What can you do? Well, you could always try one of these favorite Korean pastimes:*

- Noraebang 노래방: It's karaoke taken to a whole new level. Noraebang literally means 'singing room' and it lives up to its name. It's a private room where you and a dozen of your closest friends can sing your heart out and pound on tambourines while eating Korean snacks and swilling some soju or beer. There are comfy couches to rest or pass out on after a long night out. Noraebang is popular with the after-bar crowd, but you can do it any time of day. Have fun belting out some Queen or practice your Korean by singing the latest hit song from the Wonder Girls or Big Bang.

- If karaoke isn't your thing but you'd still like to go out and chill with some friends, try hitting up a DVD bang. They're easy to find because they'll have a big 'DVD' sign above their door. The DVD bang is the same concept as noraebang except, you guessed it, you watch DVDs instead of singing. There are thousands of titles to choose from, and there are usually a good variety of English movies mixed in with the Korean ones. You may want to go and watch some popular Korean movies as they'll usually have an English subtitle feature available.

- If you're really into computer games and you'd like to experience them on a big screen, go into any of the local PC bangs and sign up for an hour online. It's cheap and the Internet is fast and you can smoke and drink coffee as long as you want. They're all open 24 hours. There may be a wait though as they're very popular with schoolboys who want to play StarCraft after their classes are finished.

- If you want to relax, try going to a Korean sauna 사우나. Saunas are everywhere! You can always tell a sauna by its sign:

This is the universal sign of the jimjilbang. For less than ₩10,000 you can go in hot tubs, cold pools, saunas, get massages and even spend the night in their sleeping quarters (a great option for traveling on a budget).

- If you want to have a truly unique Korean experience, have a Korean friend take you out to a booking club. From the outside it'll look like a giant warehouse with lots of flashing neon lights. You'll enter through some big doors into a huge, lavish lobby. You'll then enter the main dancehall area, which is massive and packed with people. There's a stage in the front with a DJ who will play music and constantly turn it down to talk. There are tables with plush booths surrounding the dance floor on all sides. This is where it gets interesting. The whole point of a booking club is to meet people. Korean men will go to a booking club and rent a booth. They'll scan the room for girls they think are attractive. When they find one they want to talk to, they'll have their table attendant send the girl something, usually fruit or a drink. Then the attendant will tell the girl that the man who sent the gift would like to talk to them. The girl will follow the attendant back to the man's table and will sit down with him and chat. If they don't like each other, she will get up and leave. If they do, well, who knows what the night could bring? Even if it sounds a bit sleazy, it's not as bad as it sounds. Plus, it will be a Korean experience you won't easily forget!

- **Fish pedicures:** While this is not a purely Korean thing to do, it is a popular thing to do in Korea. The fish pedicure shop in Daegu was called Dr. Fish and it was hugely popular. The first time we went we actually left because we didn't want to wait over an hour for a tank. We came back on a later date and waited it out and, well, I guess it was worth it! They took us up a few stairs to a raised platform. In the floor were several long tanks full of little fish. We were instructed to roll up our pants and dip our legs into the water. Immediately the fish swim to you and start nibbling away on dead skin on your feet and legs. It's the weirdest feeling! It sort of felt like the pins and needles you feel when your foot falls asleep. I'm not sure if my feet were any smoother after we were done, but that was really not the point of Dr. Fish.

- **Karaoke Buses:** As we're learned, Koreans love their karaoke, so much so that they sometimes don't want to wait to get to their final destination before they break into song. You can actually drive around in a mobile *noraebang*, singing and playing tambourines until you get to where you're going and you can go to an actual karaoke establishment.

- **Engrish:** One of my favorite things about Asia as a whole is *Engrish.* If you don't know what Engrish is, it's basically very badly worded sentences or phrases translated from an Asian language to English onto signs or clothing. Spotting Engrish is always entertaining. I found a bag at a market in Korea that I bought in two different colors. It says: *Minutemen, Meatpuppets, Decedents, Angst.* Why? What does it mean? Why did someone decide these four words should go together? And what is a meatpuppet? The world may never know. Sometimes you'll find just bizarre sentences in reference to the subject. For instance, I was eating at Mr. Pizza, a popular Korean chain restaurant, when I noticed their slogan: *Love For Women.* Ummm....what? You can find gems like this all over, whether it's a restaurant slogan or something on a packaged snack. But the best place for Engrish is definitely a night market. They are filled with weird t-shirts that make no sense at all. I loved spotting the Engrish when I traveled through Korea and other parts of Asia.

# 10 – GETTING AROUND TOWN

*Going from having a car to not having a car is tough. It took some getting used to, especially when the weather was bad. However, just because you're without a set of wheels doesn't mean you have to walk everywhere. Korea is set up for public transport, and there are lots of cheap, no hassle options for getting around.*

- Every city, no matter how big or small, will have a local bus, usually multiple lines, going everywhere you could possibly need to go. The bus is the cheapest mode of transportation. Make sure to buy a bus card (you can get them at grocery stores or at kiosks near bus stops). You can load as much won onto them as you want and then your account will be debited each time you ride. If you pay cash each time you'll be charged more as you get discounted rates using the card. Word of warning: the buses will be packed during rush hour, so try to plan your outings during off-peak hours if you can.

- Most major cities will also have a subway line running through the city. Seoul has so many subway lines it looks like spaghetti on the map, but cities like Busan and Daegu only have a few lines. Unfortunately for me, my area did not have a subway line, so I had to take the bus or a cab anytime I wanted to go to other parts of the city, but it seemed like most people I knew lived fairly close to the subway and they were able to get downtown a lot quicker than us bus riding folk. Like the bus, the subway will also be crammed during peak hours. You can use your bus card for subway rides as well.

- Here's another 'learn from my mistakes' tip: Buy a bike. By the time I came to the conclusion that I needed a bike I was nearing the end of my time in Korea so I didn't feel it was worth the cost. You should definitely invest in one early on. Not only is it fun and a great way to burn off some energy, but just think about how much easier your trips to the grocery store will be!

- If you have the monetary means and a bit of an adventurous streak, you should look into buying a motor scooter. A lot of Koreans drive them (usually on the sidewalk, so watch out when you're a pedestrian!) and you can get a used one for a few hundred bucks. Not only will you be able to get around town faster, but you can also use them to go on weekend drives through the beautiful Korean countryside.

# 11 – LIFE IN SEOUL

*If you're living in Seoul, your life will be a bit different than what's described in this book. Think of it this way: There's Seoul then there's everywhere else in Korea. There is a reason jobs in Seoul are so competitive. There are tons of expats living in Seoul; there are a lot more dining options; there are a lot more stores offering Western goods than elsewhere in Korea; English is widely spoken; travel is easy as Incheon International Airport is just a short train ride away; there are so many subway lines going every which way that the maps look like a plate of spaghetti. You'll be able to shop at Western stores not found anywhere else in Korea. If you're in the mood for Nepalese or Mexican or Thai, you'll be able to find it. The perks of living in Seoul are endless.*

*However, you will pay a premium for living in Seoul. The cost of living is higher, the air quality is worse; there are so many people out and about at all hours of the day that it's difficult to find a place to go to get away from it all. But if you're someone who likes the big city life, Seoul is definitely your best bet.*

*This is not to say that Seoul is the only place you can live comfortably with easy access to products you're used to back home. As Korea continues to add more and more ESL positions, the demand for Western products is always rising. Most big cities will have some Western stores, you can find Western food at Costco or any big supermarket, and new non-Korean restaurants open all the time. You should have no problem finding things you want to eat and buy outside of Seoul. And if you can't find what you're looking for in your adopted hometown, hop in the KTX and take a weekend trip to Seoul to stock up on supplies and splurge on some tacos from one of the Mexican restaurants scattered across the city.*

# 12 – GROCERY SHOPPING

*During your time in Korea, you could probably get away with never having to do a serious grocery run if you don't want to. On your block there will probably be at least one orange restaurant and a handful of convenience stores, pizza or galbi joints as well. But if you like to cook at home, or you get tired of eating bibimbap and pizza every day, you'll need to venture out to the store. But don't think you have to just buy your food at the Home Plus or E-mart or Costco; there are other grocery options as well.*

- In every neighborhood there will be a local mart 마트 which will carry all the staples such as bread, drinks, eggs, vegetables and household supplies and cleaners. While they don't have nearly the selection that you'd find at a bigger store, they are quite convenient as you won't have to haul your groceries too far. Also, they have a great variety of single serving ice cream bars. In the summer I would stop by my local mart on the way home from school and buy an ice cream and it would be less than $1.

- Produce in grocery stores is expensive everywhere and Korea is no exception. However, if you can pick up fruits and vegetables at neighborhood street markets you can save a ton of money. My neighborhood had a market every Wednesday afternoon and evening, spanning about two blocks in length. I could get a whole watermelon for about ₩9,000, or a dozen oranges for ₩3,000, delicious juicy apples or Asian pears for ₩4,000. They sell more than fruit, too. You can find lots of seafood, nuts, dried fruits, even clothes and luggage! Since it's a street market, you can haggle to get a better price.

- If you're looking for a delicious loaf of bread, cake or pastries look no further than the bakery that is probably just down your street. Paris Baguette and Tous le Jours are the two biggest bakery chains in Korea and you can hardly walk a block without running into one. When I first arrived in Korea, I would buy my bread at Home Plus, but one day I decided to stop in at the Paris Baguette and I never bought another loaf of bread at the grocery store again.

# 13 – GETTING SICK

*My least favorite part about my time in Korea was how often I got sick. When you go to another country, it's full of germs that your body has never been in contact with. Add to that the fact that you'll probably be teaching young kids and you will come to the conclusion that you will get sick a lot. There's no sugarcoating it, getting sick a lot sucks. Koreans don't really believe in the concept of 'sick days'. You'll see kids with their heads down, cheeks red, sweaty, but they're still in class and they aren't going to go home. That's when you start counting down the days until you wake up with a scratchy throat and a low grade fever. It's pretty unavoidable, so I'll give you some advice for how to deal with your illnesses.*

- If you mention to a Korean that you are sick, they'll probably say you need to go to the hospital. Likewise, if they get sick, the next time you see them they'll tell you how they went to the hospital. The first time my co-teacher told me she went to the hospital the night before, I was so concerned. I asked what happened and was she okay. She looked at me like I was crazy and said of course she was okay; she just went to get antibiotics. That's when I realized that going to the hospital can also mean going to a doctor's office.

- The cold medicine found in Korean pharmacies didn't really do it for me. They're pretty weak compared with the stuff I get back at home. If you're prone to colds, you should definitely bring a few boxes of nasal decongestants with you as you may not be able to find anything strong enough to have much of an effect on your cold.

- If and when you need to take a trip to the doctor's office (or 'hospital'), they'll probably give you a prescription for antibiotics. They prescribe antibiotics for everything, it seems. After you get your prescription, you'll go back to the front desk to pay. The Korean National Health Insurance is great! Your doctor visit should be a couple of dollars, at the most. Then, you'll make your way to the pharmacy, which is usually attached to the doctor's office, either on another floor or next door. You'll give them your prescription, hang around for five minutes or so, then you'll get your Rx and, like your doctor visit, it shouldn't be more than a few dollars.

- If you're thinking that only doctor's visits are cheap and anything more serious might break the bank, think again. After only a month in Korea, I broke my foot walking up the stairs. I know, who falls *up* the stairs? Anyway, my co-teacher took me to the 'hospital' (really like an urgent care facility) to get it checked out. They put me in a wheelchair and took me back to get x-rays done on my foot. Then they fitted me for a boot and wrapped my foot and put it in the boot. Then I was given a set of crutches and was offered an injection of pain medication, which I declined due to my needle phobia. I was also given a prescription for pain medicine and, of course, antibiotics. I had two follow up visits with the doctor to check my progress over the next six weeks. Grand total for all that? A little over $50.

- Once you start meeting people who have been in Korea for a while, ask them if they have been to the doctor yet. There are usually a few English speaking doctors in bigger cities and it's definitely a lot nicer going to a doctor you can see without having to have your handler translate for you. I found a great doctor after speaking with a friend about where she went. Before I found my English speaking doctor, I had to ask my co-teacher to take me to the doctor if I needed to go. Okay, this may be TMI, but it highlights how important your privacy is when it comes to embarrassing medical issues: One time I got a yeast infection. Oddly enough, you cannot get yeast infection medication over the counter, it's prescription only. I had no idea what to do, so I had to explain my situation to my co-teacher and she made me an appointment with an OBGYN in our area. After school, she took me to the doctor's office. The doctor didn't speak English. I had to describe all of the disgusting symptoms I was having to my co-teacher, who then had to translate it into Korean to the doctor and the two nurses who were snickering as they heard what was wrong with me. The doctor was having a hard time understanding and my co-teacher didn't know the word 'yeast infection', so that went around in circles, becoming more and more embarrassing as I had to keep describing what was happening. All of this could have been avoided if I had known about the English speaking doctor who was just a few bus stops away.

- Besides the common cold and flu, there are a couple other issues that may impact your health. The first issue is mold. I knew a number of people, myself included, who had mold in their apartments. Mold is nothing to fool around with. I kept trying to treat my mold problem by myself until it became out of control, sprouting up all over all of my walls, working its way down to the floor. I finally told my co-teacher about it and, after a lot of back and forth arguing with the landlord, got the old wallpaper stripped off and had new stuff put up. Almost immediately my constant colds stopped being so frequent. My body didn't ache constantly, I didn't have congestion and sinus headaches anymore, and I felt like a new woman. I wish I had spoken up sooner.

- Something that will affect almost everyone in Korea in the spring is the dreaded yellow dust. At some point in late winter/early spring, the winds shift and yellow dust from the Gobi Desert is blown across China and Korea. It is miserable. Keep your windows closed and avoid going outside as much as possible when there's a lot of dust in the air. Even if you keep your windows sealed, the dust still somehow finds a way to get in. Everything near my windows was covered in a fine layer of dust all the time. During yellow dust season, you'll finally understand why Koreans like wearing face masks outdoors.

# 14 - HOMESICKNESS

*The hardest part of living in Korea was how incredibly homesick I would get sometimes, especially on the holidays. I remember on Christmas Day I sat in my apartment all day long watching videos on YouTube. All of my friends were out of the country on vacation, all of the stores were closed, it was too cold to want to go outside and I was so acutely aware of how alone I was. Luckily, the homesickness came in waves and would subside after a few days. It's really hard to go through, but there are some things you can do to lessen the pain:*

- Downloading Skype or other video chat systems is a must. If you're having a hard day, there's nothing better than calling someone you care about back home and getting to see their face.

- Go out to a Western restaurant. The term 'comfort food' exists for a reason. When I was down, the best pick-me-up was a meal at McDonald's or a cheese pizza at Pizza Hut.

- If you live in a city where there's a big bookstore with an English section, try getting a coffee and hanging out there. I used to do that sometimes, and just hearing your own language being spoken around you can lift your spirits.

- If you're lucky, you will meet someone with access to a US military base. I found an awesome girl on a dog sitting Facebook group who was married to a US soldier. She let my friend and I come with her on base a few times and we were able to shop at the commissary. It was like being in heaven! Everyone walking around was American, all of the products were the same things you could get at the store at home, and the fast food on base tasted exactly like home as well. It may not sound that exciting now, but when you've been deprived of certain items for an extended amount of time, the little things will excite you.

- The best thing you can do to combat the homesick blues is to go out with your friends. You need to distract yourself and fill your time with fun and adventure. Take a weekend trip to the beach or the mountains; go to the movies; splurge on a steak from Outback Steakhouse. You deserve it!

# 15 – COSTCO

*Oh Costco. There is so much I could say about this place. Whether you're in Korea, the US, Australia or anywhere in between it's the same experience: food in bulk, large crowds, long lines, cheap prices (Why yes I DO need a two pound tub of animal crackers, thank you very much. It was only $5!) Costco can be your best friend or your mortal enemy. Yeah, you got a 24 pack of Dr. Pepper on sale, but how the heck are you going to carry it back with you without breaking your shoulders?*

- The best tip I can give about Costco is bring a rolling suitcase with you. When I first started going, I would just bring a couple old Home Plus bags with me. However, waiting 15 minutes for the bus, then having to stand the whole thirty minute ride home and then braving the mile long walk from the bus stop to my apartment was so backbreaking. One day I decided to bring my suitcase for a particularly ambitious shopping trip and it was such a great decision. For the first time, I woke up the day after my Costco trip without having a sore neck and back!

- Do not, under any circumstances, go to Costco on the weekends unless you absolutely have to. It is absolutely maddening. Going to Costco is a family affair, and there will be three or four generations of family there together, all plodding around, browsing without a care in the world, blocking your access to the ₩7,000 bacon sale. If you go on a weekend and want to eat at the food court, be prepared to sit on the floor. It's a madhouse and it will take about twenty minutes just to get your food, and unless you tag team and have someone save a table, you'll be standing around helplessly while your food gets cold. One time I ate lunch on the floor and on Monday one of my students came up to me and said he saw me at Costco and why was I sitting on the floor? I didn't have a good answer for that.

• Lines do not exist at the Costco food court on the weekends. It's a nice concept, but the mob of people sort of takes on a mind of its own and the line turns into something akin to a mosh pit at a concert. Expect pushing, cutting in line, and excessive amounts of people not knowing what to order when they finally get up to the counter.

• Don't bother getting free samples. Everyone loves free food and if there's a sample cart set up you will hardly even be able to get down the aisle, let alone actually get a free sample. A blog post I wrote about this issue at the time is absolutely perfect, so I will share it with you: Last week they were giving samples of cheesecake. They had a sign up saying 'be patient, we are preparing the samples' and there were DOZENS of people standing there and the second the poor Costco worker took the sign away they were attacked from all sides, people grabbing samples. It looked like Black Friday times a million. There were probably 25 little cups of cheesecake and it was like a shark feeding frenzy. Within 20 seconds all of the cups were gone.

*Today, they were giving free samples of cookies. Not even whole cookies, just little broken pieces of cookies. I saw this teenage girl literally mow over an old woman to get to the sample tray. She shoved this little old lady to the side, causing her to almost topple over, while the girl went to get her cookie crumb.*

# 16 – TRAVELING KOREA

*Korea's size and great public transportation options make traveling throughout the country easy and affordable. For months, my friends and I would take a trip to a different area of the country every weekend. You can spend one weekend shopping at high end malls and dancing in Seoul and the next weekend you could be riding bikes through ancient burial mounts from the Silla dynasty in Gyeongju (my favorite weekend trip!) While travel may be easy, it's still nice to have some sort of idea what to expect before you show up at the bus or train station:*

- Korail is Korea's national train system. There are three different types of trains: There's the KTX, which is the high speed train that can get from Seoul to Busan in less than three hours. The mid-range train is called Saemaeul 새마을, which still bills itself as an express train because there are not as many stops but the top speed is much slower than the KTX. The slow train, Mungunghua 무궁화 is frustratingly slow and stops at almost every station, but if you're going to a small town, this may be your only option. The KTX will run you around ₩50,000 for Seoul to Busan, and cheaper if you're getting on somewhere in between. The Mungunghua will cost less than half that, although you may spend most of your day getting to your final destination. You can find train schedules and pricing at korail.com, which will also be in the links section at the end of the book.

- If you're looking to travel on a budget, taking a bus is the way to go. Every city, no matter how big or small, will have a bus station with multiple inter-country buses leaving day and night. The buses are generally comfortable and can offer you the chance to see more of the Korean countryside than you would have on the train.

- I mentioned earlier that you should print out bus and subway routes for your city when you first move to Korea. The same advice applies here. If you're traveling to a different city that has a subway line, you might want to print out a map. Yes, there are maps in the stations, but sometimes it's nice to have something else as a reference as well.

- If you're traveling to a different city and aren't able to stay with friends, but worry about the cost of staying in a hotel, fear not! Seoul has a plethora of affordable hostels which are close to areas where foreigners tend to congregate. You may have a hard time finding a hostel outside of Seoul, but you could always consider staying in a jimjilbang, a Korean spa. They're open 24 hours and have sleeping areas available. Another affordable option is to stay at a love motel. I know what you're thinking; ewww gross! But love motels in Korea are a bit different from what you are probably used to hearing about back home. Because Koreans tend to marry in their late 20s and don't usually move out of their parents houses until they're married, young couples frequent love motels to have some privacy. While that thought might make you squeamish, at least take comfort in the fact that they're not used by crack addicts and hookers like in the west. A love motel with a good reputation can be a great place to stay with a few friends as you explore.

# 17 – TRAVELING OUTSIDE OF KOREA

*One of the best things about living in Korea is the ease of getting to travel to other exotic places outside of Korea. Flights to Japan and China are less than 3 hours long and you can get to the Philippines and other destinations in Southeast Asia in a half day instead of the day and a half it would take from the Americas, Europe and Africa.*

- International travel from South Korea is not as cheap as you'd imagine. Before I went over, I had dreams of flying over to Tokyo for a long weekend or a concert. Then I looked at the ticket prices. Over ₩400,000 for such a short flight?! That's nuts! I never did end up going to Japan, although I wish I had now that I'm back home. Flights from Seoul to Beijing are cheap, but travel to China requires a visa which could end up being more expensive than the plane ticket (at least for Americans). There are some budget airlines that serve Korea now. Air Asia, Jin Air and Cebu Pacific are all lower cost carriers that travel to destinations in Southeast Asia and the Philippines.

- In recent years, as more airlines have been allowed to serve Korea, the cost of international travel has come down quite a bit, but it can still be pricy depending on the time of year. Most schools take their breaks around the same time, so if you want to travel on your school vacations be prepared to pay a lot more than during the school year.

- If you fly into Incheon and need to make your way to Seoul Station to catch the KTX back to your home city, look into taking a bus from the airport to the train station instead of a cab. It's a long ride and a cab will cost you close to a hundred dollars. Unless you're traveling with a big group of people who can split the cost, you're better off taking the bus. The bus is cheap and you can buy tickets right outside of the arrival hall. The only downside is you may have to wait for the next bus to arrive and you'll have a few stops along the way, so if you're in a time crunch you it may be worth it to shell out the extra money to jump in a cab and go.

- Bring plenty of cash or a credit card from home-many Korean ATM cards will not work overseas.

# 18 – INTERACTING WITH K-TEACHERS

*If you have a Korean co-teacher to work with, it can be the most rewarding - and challenging - relationship you'll have in Korea. They can be your best friend...or your worst enemy. Sometimes you just aren't lucky and you have to work with a co-teacher you can't stand, and they can't stand you. But most of the time your co-teachers will be enthusiastic about getting to know you and your culture better, and are more than willing to teach you about theirs. No matter how much you and your Korean co-teachers get along, navigating the Korean school system's waters is always tricky, but with the right knowledge you can have a much smoother experience.*

- You will probably hear that you should bring little gifts from home to give to your co-teachers when you first arrive in Korea. This is great advice. It's a small gesture that will go a long way towards good will. I brought my co-teachers key chains and cute candles from home. It cost me all of $10 and they were very appreciative.

- Koreans are gift givers by nature, so you will probably get a lot of little things from them over the year or two you are there, especially when it comes to food. I'd recommend bringing in snacks from time to time to return the favor. The first couple times I brought snacks to my co-teachers, I brought muffins from Costco and then some sort of pastries from Paris Baguette. They appreciated the gesture, but I could tell that they didn't really want to eat it. The next time, I brought in some oranges and they were all over that. Then I brought in pears and again, it was a hit. I learned over my time there, from experience and from talking to Korean friends, that a lot of Koreans aren't really into sweets. Of course this is not saying that no Koreans like sweets, but in general if you can bring in a healthy, light snack it will probably be better received than a heavy, high calorie snack.

- Rice cakes. Koreans love them. You, however, probably won't. I think I knew one foreign teacher who actually liked them. They are not the same rice cakes that we have in the West. They're gooey squares of chewy, firm rice substance. I don't know how else to describe them, I really don't. Koreans love to bring them as gifts and as snacks for the break room. Try to choke down a bite or two to be polite.

- At some point during your employment at your school (especially if you're in a public school), you will have to attend some after school outings with the entire staff of your school. These are almost always at Korean style barbeque or seafood restaurants where the food is plentiful and the booze is always flowing. The male teachers will want you to do shots of soju with them. Even the principal will probably want you to do shots with him. Be careful. Once you start drinking, you will be expected to continue drinking until everyone is finished. This could mean a long night hugging your toilet and a massive hangover in the morning. I didn't want this to happen, so I (truthfully) said I didn't like to drink alcohol often and I would toast with a cup of water instead of a shot of soju. But if you do decide to drink, just know that you'll probably be getting pretty wasted. In Korea, if a glass is empty, someone will refill it. If you want to have one drink to be polite, just drink half of it. That way nobody will come around and refill your glass without you knowing it.

- As we learned earlier, Koreans are really into karaoke. A lot of these teacher dinners end with a stop at the local noraebang. If you like karaoke and you want to go, great! But if you don't, this is a great opportunity to use the foreigner card. As a foreign teacher, you'll have a lot more leeway in these types of situations. Whereas the Korean teachers are expected to stay out late drinking, even if they don't want to, the foreign teachers have a pass to go home early.

# 19 - PETS

*Most of us at one time or another has had a pet of some sort. Some of still have pets, or would like to have one. Some people worry whether that's possible when going over to Korea. The answer is yes, but...*

- It's certainly possible to bring your cat or dog from home with you to Korea. You'll need to have a recent checkup and some sort of documentation from your veterinarian saying they're healthy to get them into the country. However, not all apartments will allow you to have a pet and many times it's impossible to know whether your apartment is pet friendly or not until you get there.

- If you do bring your pet, or plan to adopt one while in Korea, keep in mind that your apartment will likely be extremely small and barely enough space for you, let alone your German shepherd or a stinky cat box. You'll have to decide whether it's fair to you and your animal to be in such cramped quarters for a year or more.

- If you decide to adopt an animal in Korea, look into getting one from one of the animal shelters around the country instead of a pet store. Unlike western countries, there isn't a lot of funding for animal shelters and most rely on the generosity of private donors. The facilities are very bare and basic, with dogs being kept in small metal cages with nothing but a sheet of newspaper to sleep on. Most of these animals will eat up affection and have so much love to give. As I said earlier, I adopted a little Shih Tzu-pug mix from the animal shelter in Daegu. She was so sweet and loving and I couldn't let her spend her life in the shelter. When I adopted her, the shelter cut her hair and bathed her and I was able to see how skinny she was. You could count her ribs! After a few months of love and proper meals, she had gained weight and was ready for a life of being spoiled back home in America. She's the best dog anyone could ask for and I couldn't recommend adopting a shelter dog enough.

- You can get pet supplies from chain stores, specialty pet stores, and even the Daiso dollar stores!

- If you'd like to have a pet but aren't ready for the commitment of owning a cat or dog, you can get fish, hamsters and bunnies from the chain stores like Home Plus or Emart.

## Words to Know for Dining Out and Taking Taxis

**Kamsahabnida** – Thank you
**"_____ Juseyo"** - _____ please (For instance, mul juseyo means 'water please')
**Gesanso juseyo** – check please
**Oenjjok (pronounced 'Wench-o)** – left
**Oreunjjok (pronounced 'Oran-cho)** – right
**Jigjin (pronounced chi-chin)** – straight
**Yeogie (pronounced yo-gi)** - here

# 20 – YOUR KOREAN STUDENTS

*Sometimes it's easy to forget that you're going to Korea to teach English because you're so busy thinking about traveling and trying new things, but really, your students are the reason you're there. Teaching English may be the most rewarding job you'll ever have, but it can also be difficult and frustrating as you have to deal with the language and cultural barriers in place. However, with a little bit of skill and a lot of patience, you will really enjoy your job. I won't give much advice on classroom management or lesson plans, because it's something you really need to learn through experience, but there is more to teaching ESL than what happens during your class.*

- Your students will be curious about you. If you're in a rural area you may be the first foreign teacher they've ever had. Put together a nice PowerPoint slideshow about yourself and where you came from to show your students on the first day of class. They'll be really excited to see pictures of your life.

- Expect to say "hello" about a thousand times a day, at school and outside of school. I don't think a single day went by where kids weren't screaming 'hello!!!' when they saw me. Another common variation is "Hello, nice to meet you!" even if they've met you before and have class with you twice a week. To be honest, it gets a little bit annoying but the students are just excited to get to practice some English phrases.

- Your students may give you gifts throughout the year. Sometimes I would get food, sometimes cute drawings, and my favorite student actually got me a Christmas ornament of the Korean flag. It goes up on my tree every year.

- Don't give your phone number to your students - they WILL call you.

- Try not to let your students see where you live either. I had two students who followed me home one day and found that they lived down the street from me. Almost every day they would come by my house and ring the doorbell and call my phone. Luckily the door to get into my apartment building was protected with a passcode or they would have been knocking on my door. They are quite persistent and won't give up easily!

- Try to do nice things for your students if you can. During our school's hour lunch, there would be students in the classroom playing with the English games. Sometimes I would come out of my office and play with them. The girls who lived on my street would try to walk home with me after school, and on hot days I would take them to the local mart and buy them a drink or an ice cream. Something as simple as that really made their day!

- Korean children are under tremendous pressure from their parents and from society to excel at school. From the moment they enter elementary school, they are being prepped for college entrance exams. I tried to keep this in mind when my classes were hard to manage. English class is sometimes the only class your students will have that doesn't weigh heavily on their future, so some kids use that as their time to slack off. It's good to remember that they aren't being bad or disrespectful because of anything you've done wrong.

- If you are able to incorporate art projects into your English class you should definitely take advantage of that opportunity. As I said previously, Korean classes have very rigid structures and focus heavily on preparing for standardize testing. Art and creativity are not highly valued in Korean schools. A lot of my students really enjoyed doing activities such as drawing comics or pictures in class because it was the only chance they had to do such things. I once had a class of third graders during winter camp where I printed out pictures of sea creatures like fish and lobsters for the camp kids to color. Some of the students just sat there looking at the paper. I asked why they weren't coloring. They said they didn't know how; coloring was too hard. I didn't quite know how to respond to that!

- Remember this word: ANJDA (pronounced ahn-ja). It means 'sit' in Korean. I found that the kids were more intimidated by me yelling that in Korean rather than in English.

- If you're black, your students may think you're from Africa or Jamaica or related to Barack Obama. I had several black friends from various countries whose students said both of those things to them when they first began teaching. My American friends also said that their students didn't believe they were American because they were black.

**Where You're From**

**Miguk 미국인** – America
**Hoju 호주** – Australia
**Kaenada 캐나다** – Canada
**Yeong-gug 영국** – England
**Aillaendeu 아일랜드** – Ireland
**Seukoteullaendeu 스코틀랜드** – Scotland
**Nam-apeulika goghwagug 남아프리카 공화국** – South Africa

# 21 – GET FESTIVE

*Koreans love a good festival. At any given time, there is at least one festival going on somewhere in Korea. Whatever you're interested in, chances are they'll have a festival celebrating it. Like fabric? There's a festival for that. Like ceramics? There's a festival for that? Feel like celebrating rice? Yes, there's even a festival for that as well. Korea has so many festivals it can be hard to choose what to see. Here is a list of what I think are the most interesting festivals for foreigners to attend:*

- **Busan World Fireworks Festival**: Held in October, this festival is basically the Korean version of a 4th of July fireworks celebration. Get some friends and a cooler of soju or Hite and head down to Gwangalli Beach in Busan and take in the amazing fireworks that are set off from the ocean. If one fireworks festival just isn't enough for you, check out the Pohang International Fireworks Festival in late July through early August.

- **Andong International Maskdance Festival**: More commonly known as the Andong Mask Festival, this is one of the more popular festivals for Koreans and foreigners alike. Held in

Andong (obviously) in late September and early October, you can see traditional Korean masks, as well as masks from other Asian countries. Performers will wear the masks and put on dramatic dances to match the type of mask they're wearing.

- **Hwacheon Sancheoneo Ice Festival**: The most popular winter festival is the Ice Festival which takes place in the rural Gangwon-do Province throughout the month of January. See amazing ice carvings, go sledding or even ice fishing. Just make sure to bring a thick jacket!

- **Korean Food Festival**: The Korean Food Festival is held in Jeonju (the bibimbap capitol of the country) in October. There are different tasting areas all over town where you can sample different Korean delicacies or even learn to cook some Korean dishes yourself. The Jeonju Bibimbap Festival is held at the same time during this event. My mouth is watering just thinking about it.

- My absolute favorite festival is the **Jinhae Cherry Blossom Festival**. The dates change year to year based on when the cherry blossoms are expected to bloom, but it's usually late March or early April and runs for a couple weeks until the trees lose their flowers. The entire city of Jinhae is just inundated with pinkish white cherry blossoms-and tourists. The festival is probably the most popular in the country, and for good reason. Take in the sights and smells, and you can even have some cherry blossom ice cream on a warm day. Get to the train station early if you're going on a weekend; the trains to Jinhae sell out fast this time of year.

- **Haeundae Sand Festival**: The Haeundae Sand Festival is a great way to kick off your Korean summer. Busan's most popular beach hosts a large array of incredible sand sculptures, as well as beach volleyball matches and a running race. This festival takes place in early June, before monsoon season officially begins.

- **Seoul Lotus Lantern Festival**: This festival celebrates Buddha's birthday by lighting up Seoul with over 100,000 paper lanterns. Take in the beautiful colors of the lanterns along the Han River, enjoy food vendors located on decorated streets, learn about Buddhism and even make your own lantern as you wait for the grand finale, the Lotus Lantern Parade. The festival takes place in May.

- **Boryeong Mud Festival**: Perhaps the most well-known festival among the expat crowd, the Boryeong Mud Fest is exactly how it sounds - muddy. In the heart of monsoon season, the quiet coastal town of Boryeong is transformed into a muddy, mayhem filled, non-stop party. Expect to get wet, dirty, and probably drunk. To be honest, you will probably either love Mud Fest or hate it. I, for one, did not really enjoy it. If you're really into partying hard and drinking for two days straight, you'll definitely have a good time. If that's not really your thing, you might wonder why you spent ₩200,000 to hang out on a rainy beach with a bunch of drunk foreigners, eating overpriced Korean barbeque and sharing a tiny room in a love motel with four other people.

# 22 - ENTERTAINMENT

- When I moved to Korea, the idea of going out to see movies never entered my mind. I couldn't speak the language, so why would I go to a movie? I was proven wrong though the first time I walked past a movie theater and saw that about half of the movies listed were Hollywood movies, with Hollywood actors, in ENGLISH! It was very exciting. What made it all even more exciting was that movie tickets are much, much less expensive than any theaters I've seen in any Western country I've been to. I would pay about $7 for a ticket.

- If you're a music lover, there's no shortage of concerts in Seoul. A lot of big western performers stop in Seoul, and the tickets are priced similarly to what you would pay at a concert back home. If you don't live in Seoul, you'll have to commute to see most Western acts as that's usually the only South Korean stop artists make. If money's not an issue, you could also fly over to Japan to catch some shows that may not stop in Korea.

- There is an exception to the rule that most artists on world tours don't stop anywhere in Korea besides Seoul. That exception is the Jisan Valley Music Festival. Held on the last weekend of July at Jisan Forest Resort, the festival features dozens of famous and up and coming rock bands from the West as well as Korean performers. The Jisan Valley Music Festival is organized like any other music festival you would find back home-multiple stages set up and an entire weekend of music. You can get a ticket for one day of music or a three day pass. Camping is available for those who want to stay all weekend.

- For those of you wanting to stay closer to home (or not shell out as much won to hear live music), there are loads of local bands, both expat and Korean, that play in small clubs on the weekends. If you're musically inclined, perhaps you could even form your own expat band and tour Korea's clubs on the weekends!

# 23 – KOREA HAS FOUR DISTINCT SEASONS

*The mantra 'Korea has four distinct seasons' will be repeated to you many times during your stay in the country. But what does that mean for you? Well, I'll tell you:*

- **Summer**: Summers in Korea are brutally hot, so head out to the coast to take a dip on the ocean. However, avoid the popular beach spots as they get crowded in a way you can't imagine (do a Google Image search for *Haeundae Beach in Summer…*) You could also brave water theme parks such as Caribbean Bay in the Seoul area, although the crowds will be similar to the beach. Summer is also a great time to take in a Korean Major League Baseball game. The stadiums in Korea are a lot less strict than you may be used to back home, so you can bring in your own food and drinks. Eat, drink and be merry with your friends as you root for your (semi) home team.

- **Fall**: Fall is the most perfect few weeks you will experience in Korea. After the oppressive heat of the summer, the cool, crisp air will refresh your soul and energize you to get out and explore. Go on a hike through the mountains near your home and enjoy the fall colors; head out to Gyeongju and take a bike ride; spend a weekend in Seoraksan, Korea's tallest mountain and arguably the best place to see fall colors. Plan a trip to tour the DMZ before the cold weather sets in around November; maybe join an expat flag football league. Fall was so wonderful, especially for someone like me whose home in America doesn't get an autumn. Every day after school I would go on walks for hours, checking out the colorful leaves in every part of town I could get to. It was truly a wonderful couple of weeks.

- **Winter**: Winter in Korea can vary greatly - in the northern part of the country, there will be cold temperatures and snow. In Daegu, where I lived, we had some of the coldest temperatures in the country but it only snowed a handful of times. In the southern part of Korea and Jeju Island, winter is fairly mild. In the northern mountains, there is enough snow to support several large ski resorts (the 2018 Winter Olympics will be held in Pyeongchang, to give you an idea of how good the winter sports conditions can be). There are twelve popular ski resorts where you can ski and snowboard to your heart's content. It can be tricky to ski in Korea though, as there are many people on the slopes and a lot of them stand around in the middle of the run chatting while skiers have to navigate around them. If you're a novice skier like I am, this is problematic. I wasn't able to control my speed well enough and had to purposely fall in order to avoid running into someone. I ended up having to get rescued by ski patrol as the slopes were closing before I made it to the bottom. It was very embarrassing! The slopes reopen in the early evening for night skiing, but I spent the rest of the evening in the lodge snacking and drinking hot drinks with some friends. Also, try to arrange accommodation before you arrive. We decided to wing it and find a place to stay once we arrived in Muju, but everything was sold out! Thankfully we met another group of foreigners at the train station who had a room and we were able to stay with them. If you're not into the great outdoors but you like to golf, go to one of the many screen golf places in your town (I guarantee you there will be one nearby.)

- **Spring**: After a long, hard winter nothing is more uplifting than that first sprig of green leaves popping up on the bare branches of the trees in your neighborhood. Now that the weather is getting warmer, you'll want to go outside and be active again. Spring expat baseball and softball leagues begin practicing and it's a great way to exercise and socialize. Go to one of the many spring festivals that pop up around the country. Volunteer to walk dogs at the animal shelter. Work on shedding some of the pounds you may have gained during your semi-hibernation during the winter. Go for hikes to see the cherry and apricot blossoms in March and April. Find a lake or river nearby that has duck paddle boats and get a group of friends together for an afternoon of fun. During the spring, my group of friends and I would gather most weekends and try new restaurants in new areas of town we hadn't been yet.

# 24 – HELPFUL HINTS AND TIPS

- Carry some hand sanitizer with you when you go out. A lot of public restrooms did not have soap (or else it was a bar of soap that was covered in dirt and hair). I also kept a dispenser of sanitizer at my desk at school as the bathrooms there would frequently run out of soap.

- I would also recommend carrying a small packet of tissues with you when you're out, especially if you're traveling. You will sometimes encounter restrooms that don't have any toilet paper.

- Get used to using squat toilets. In Korea, there are a lot of places that have Western style toilets, but an equal if not greater amount of places that only have squat toilets. Once you get over the initial unease of using them, you may prefer them to throne style toilets. Just make sure to squat the right direction!

- Koreans pretty much exclusively use Internet Explorer and most banking websites aren't compatible with any other browser. If you're having trouble with online banking, check to make sure you're using IE before you punch a hole in your screen.

- Most people I knew in Korea lost a lot of weight. I know I did! Between eating healthier food and walking everywhere, you will most likely lose weight and tone up. That was definitely my favorite part about being a pedestrian in Korea.

- If you're a Christian, you'll be happy to know that you can still attend church in English if you live in or near a major city.

# 25 – THINGS TO GET USED TO

*No matter where you're from in the West, Korea will be a shock to your senses at some point or another. Unless you've lived in an Asian country before, there will be a lot of things that make you scratch your head or shake your head.*

- Spitting is something you must get used to wherever you go in Korea. Old men are the worst offenders, but it's something that almost everyone does. People spit in the street and on the sidewalks. Several times I saw students spit on the floor of the classroom. I saw an old lady spit on the floor of the bus. I've seen spit on subways and the trains. It's very unappealing, but just one of those things you have to learn to get used to.

- Pushing and shoving out in public is something else you need to get used to, unless you come from a big city back home where this is the norm as well. Anytime you're in a crowded public place, you're bound to encounter some pushing and shoving. As I mentioned earlier, Costco is always a jostling experience. I found that the ones who shove the most are old ladies. They don't let anyone stop them from getting where they need to go as quickly as possible! The worst time for this is when you're getting onto a bus or a train. Sometimes there will be a little old lady who literally knocks people aside with her purse, cuts in front of them in line, and shoves the next person aside so she can get onto the bus or train first and get a good seat.

- Did you know that sleeping with a fan on overnight can cause death? No? Well you are certainly going to learn about it when you go to Korea, whether a Korean tells you about it or you hear a foreigner talking about it. Fan death is probably the most ridiculous thing you will hear in Korea. If you buy an electric fan in a store, it will always have a timer on it so you can make sure it turns off at some point during the night. The causes of fan death include hypothermia and asphyxiation. Nobody is really sure how the fan death theory started to spread. Some people think it's an excuse to cover up suicides or alcohol poisoning, other theories say that it's actually carbon dioxide poisoning from the *ondol* (under floor heating system in Korea), which in rural areas is used by lighting coals under the floor to heat the room. No matter how crazy it sounds, it's definitely a real Korean superstition.

- I don't consider my hometown to be the cleanest place in the world, but I was shocked at how much garbage is in the streets in Korea. Even though Korean cities have been trying to make positive changes by installing trashcans in downtown areas, you still won't be able to walk a block without seeing some sort of trash littering the road. There was an empty lot beside the bus stop in my neighborhood, and the amount of trash that had been thrown over the chain-link fence was appalling. You do eventually get used to seeing food wrappers and cigarette butts everywhere you go, but it definitely takes away from the beauty of the place.

- What could be more obnoxious than a truck that drives around blaring loud advertisements for products or political candidates?

A truck that drives around your neighborhood at seven in the morning blaring loud advertisements. These trucks are called Bongo trucks and they're extremely annoying. There's usually a guy standing in the bed of the little truck shouting into a microphone. If it's a political advertisement, sometimes the candidates are the ones doing the shouting while a bunch of dancing girls surround him and pulsating dance music blasts in the background. Good times.

• Construction is a constant part of life in Korea. If there is construction going on in your area, expect to be jarred awake every morning before seven by jackhammers and noisy machines running.

• People wearing surgical masks doesn't sound quite as strange as it looks. Imagine you're standing in front of your class and nearly all of your students are wearing masks covering the bottom half of their faces. You can't even really tell who is saying what. And imagine walking down the street on a crowded Saturday afternoon, a lone foreigner in a sea of Koreans who look like dental assistants. They usually wear the masks in the winter to prevent the spread of germs, which isn't such a bad idea except people are always going to get colds in the winter. However, the face mask does have a less known side effect - it will keep your face warm on cold days! I got good use out of mine that way.

• Winters can be frigid in Korea, but that doesn't stop the schools from opening all their windows while the heaters are on full blast.

• Koreans have a very different idea of what good toppings for pizza are. They're quite fond of pizza with corn and sweet potatoes as toppings. Some have sweet potatoes in the crust, some have sweet potato puree covering the dough, and all seem to have corn. I have no idea who decided to put these ingredients together for the first time, but Koreans love this mixture. Most of my friends did not care for this pizza, but I found it to be okay. Not great, but definitely edible. You'll also find shrimp pizza, spam pizza, seafood pizza, cream cheese filled crust, and even pizza with cheese sauce drizzled on top.

- On the subject of food, the chip aisle at the grocery store is full of shrimp flavored chips. They weren't as disgusting as they sound, but I certainly did not eat them voluntarily (a student shoved one in my mouth one day so I had to eat it). You can find shrimp mixed in with almost any kind of food. Shrimp pizza; shrimp cookies; shrimp burgers…you get the idea.

- Korean bakeries love to ruin perfectly good bread by sprinkling sugar on them or filling them with beans. I will never forget the day I was on the DMZ tour: my friend bought a package of garlic bread from a convenience store bakery for us to snack on. It looked delicious and I was starving. I took a big bite and almost spit the bread out. It was covered with sugar! Who eats garlic bread with sugar on top? Koreans do. They're also a big fan of filling pastries with sweet red bean paste, which is definitely an acquired taste.

- The hardest thing to get used to is friends coming and going. Every day in Korea people are finishing contracts and leaving, while just as many new people are arriving for their new contracts. You can make some amazing friends, only to have to say goodbye to them a few months later.

# THIS IS KOREA: EPILOGUE

In the beginning you measure time in years. *One year left. I'll be in Korea for a year.* Then after you're settled in, the countdown turns to months. *I still have ten months left in Korea.* It sounds like such a long time, no matter how great of a time or how horrible of a time you are having. Sometimes that time will feel like a jail sentence. *I still have to be in Korea for nine more months!* Sometimes I would hit a real rough patch, like when my childhood cat died halfway through my contract. I couldn't even think of the future; I was just focused on surviving one day at a time. Most everyone will have a phase like this and, as clichéd as this sounds, it will pass. Trust me. As soon as you book that ticket out of Korea, that countdown sounds less like a jail sentence and more like a timer where a buzzer will go off at the end; the monthly countdown turns into a weekly one. *Oh my god, I can't believe I only have twelve weeks left in Korea!* You'll start trying to run through the items on your Korean bucket list every weekend. You just *have* to spend a day out on the lake in swan boats. You'll go to that baseball game with your friends even if it's supposed to rain all night. Then, as you watch the number of weeks shrink, the countdown switches to mere days. *What? I only have thirty days left in Korea, how can this be?* You start going downtown for *galbi* dinners with friends even though it's a school night. You'll go all the way across the city to try that *samgyupsal* place your Korean friends rave about. You'll stay up later than you want to every weekend because you have to make the most of your last few days in Korea. Maybe you should have gone to that K-pop concert in Seoul after all; that bubblegum pop is starting to grow on you.

Sometimes I still can't believe I'm back in America. I remember planning my move to Korea for over a year before I actually went. While I was there, sometimes it felt like it would never end. But it did. I remember the last day in my apartment; it was madness. I had not budgeted my time well and I spent too much time going out with friends and not enough time getting organized to leave (while it was stressful, it was absolutely the right decision!) I made a few frantic, last minute post office runs to ship stuff home, I took out multiple bags of trash to the curb, I was on my hands and knees scrubbing the grout in the shower trying to make my place as clean as possible for my replacement.

I looked at the clock on my phone. It was three, time to go if I was going to make the train down to Busan. I packed the last few belongings I was keeping, then took a deep breath and picked up my suitcase. There was nothing left to do. My Korean apartment, which I had grown to love despite its mold problems and small kitchen, was not my home anymore. I walked around slowly, taking mental pictures of every last detail. I knew I would never be here again. I thought I would get emotional, but I was so exhausted I was numb. I picked up my suitcase and duffel bag, then walked out the door. Before I shut the door, I turned and looked one last time at my former home, then I closed the door for the last time.

I hailed a taxi on the street and wedged my suitcase in the small trunk. I told him to take me to Dongdaegu Station. For some reason, he took the long way out of my neighborhood. It was almost as if he knew I was leaving for good. We drove down my street, then turned right at the rice paddy and headed towards Palgan Mountain. I looked longingly at the rice paddy that had been my sanctuary and my happy place while I lived in Daegu. Soon, that too was out of sight.

I arrived at the train station and bought my ticket, then boarded the KTX for Busan Station. I was exhausted, but forced myself to stay awake as we pulled out of Daegu. A lump formed in my throat as the train passed the last parts of the city and entered the rural area to the south. The rice paddies were tall and green and farmers were working hard in the fields. I eventually drifted off into a light sleep, and only woke up once I heard the Korean string instrumental version of The Beatles 'Let it Be', which played when the train arrived at a station.

I took the subway to a faraway suburb of Busan where my friend lived. He was flying out to the Philippines with me that evening. At that point I think I was still in denial. My mind could not grasp the fact that this was the end.

After a dinner of chicken wings, my friend and I hauled our suitcases downstairs and caught a cab to the Busan airport. I checked in for my flight on Cebu Pacific Air. Unfortunately, my friend forgot his passport at his apartment and had to rebook his flight for later that week. I had to say a quick goodbye to him as my flight was boarding soon.

I went through immigration and the customs agent made me turn in my alien registration card. That's when it hit me-I'm really leaving.

I had no time to sit around as the flight began boarding when I exited customs. I took my seat in the rear of the plane next to the window. It was after 9pm and I couldn't see beyond the airport runway, save for the lights coming from homes in the distant mountains.

After what seemed like an hour, the plane left the gate and taxied to the runway. I stared out the window as we took off and climbed into the clouds far above Busan. I watched as the lights of South Korea grow smaller and smaller until they looked like little stars in a faraway galaxy. I didn't want to leave but I had to go. I turned away from the window and looked forward. The world was waiting.

# LINKS YOU SHOULD SAVE

While this guide was created to give you an overview of many different facets of Korean life, you can still gain a lot of useful knowledge by doing some research online. I have created a list of links for you which you may find helpful. They have been organized by topic.

## Travel
*Find and book train travel throughout Korea*
http://info.korail.com/2007/eng/eng_index.jsp
*Official Korea Tourism website. Learn about destinations, food, hotels and general travel information*
http://english.visitkorea.or.kr/enu/index.kto

## Lesson Plans
*The absolute best place to find lesson plans. If you're feeling uninspired or you get a last minute class or camp dumped on you, this is the place to go.*
http://www.waygook.org/

## Currency Conversion
www.xe.com

## Advice
*The Korean Job Discussion Forums at Dave's ESL Café can be a very informative place where you can ask questions and get answers from ESL veterans. Just take most comments with a grain of salt...*
http://forums.eslcafe.com/korea/index.php

**Post Office**
http://www.koreapost.go.kr/eng/main/index.jsp

**Lifestyle**
*Supplements, vitamins and health foods can be difficult to find, but you can order them on iherb and have them shipped to your house or school.*
http://www.iherb.com
*Love reading but don't live near a bookstore with a decent English language section? Check out What the Book, which is based in Seoul. You can browse thousands of titles and have them shipped to you.*
http://www.whatthebook.com
*If you love to shop online and worry about having to give that up, fear not! G market is the Korean version of eBay. Find everything from clothes to skin care to entertainment on this one-stop e-shop.*
http://global.gmarket.co.kr/Home/Main

Made in the USA
San Bernardino, CA
15 December 2015